Spike & Zola

Spike &Zola

PATTERNS Designed for Laughter...

and Appliqué, Painting or Stenciling

by Donna French Collins

American Quilter's Society

P. O. Box 3290 • Paducah, KY 42002-3290

Designed by
Donna French Collins & Kelly Cooper Collins

Illustrations & Lettering by
Kelly Cooper Collins

Fabrics Hand-dyed by
Edith Tanniru of American Beauty Fabrics

Hand appliqué & quilting by
Donna French Collins

Library of Congress Cataloging-in-Publicaton Data

Collins, Donna French
    Spike & Zola : patterns designed for laughter, and appliqué,
painting or stenciling / by Donna French Collins.
            p.   cm.
    ISBN 0-89145-828-X : $9.95
        1. Patchwork–Patterns.   I. Title.   II. Title: Spike and Zola.
TT835.C6473   1993
746.44'5041–dc20
                                                                93-34458
                                                                CIP

Additional copies of this book may be ordered from:

American Quilter's Society
P.O. Box 3290
Paducah, KY 42002-3290
@9.95. Add $1.00 for postage and handling.

Dedicated to my friend Brenda
and all of the other
flamingo lovers out there

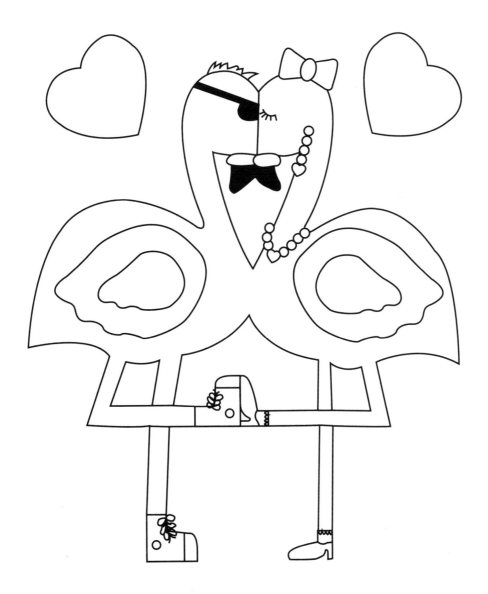

TABLE OF CONTENTS

My first Spike & Zola quilt was composed of 12 blocks, each representing one month of the year. In the blocks these two flamingos and their cute little critter friends were "caught" in a variety of amusing scenes.

I soon found people who saw my work wanted to use these designs for their own quilts, and for placemats, sweatshirts, children's clothing, tote bags, and a host of other textile projects. Some people just wanted drawings of the designs to share this "flamingo humor" with their friends.

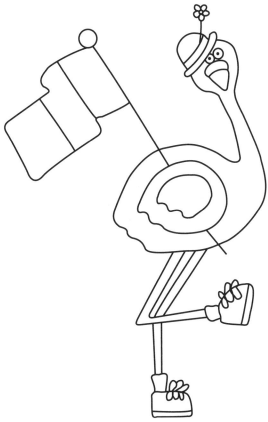

This book can become whatever you want — a humorous gift book for a special friend; a coloring book for young or adult fun; a pattern resource for anyone who appliqués, stencils, or paints; or a pattern book for my Spike & Zola quilts.

It provides full-size patterns which you can use for a 12-block quilt, or a 4-block wall hanging, or any other project. You can use parts of the designs, or even the smaller drawings at the front. Your imagination and creativity can lead you anywhere!

Regardless of the use you choose, you are sure to have great fun with Spike & Zola. The patterns truly are designed for laughter as much as for appliqué, painting and stenciling!

BRRR, THE FIRE'S OKAY, BUT THE QUILT SAVED THE DAY!

ARTIFICIAL LOVE, YOU CAN BE SURE THIS ONE WON'T GET AWAY!

HOP, MARCH, SLITHER . . . HOP, MARCH, SLITHER . . .

HEY SPIKE, WILL YOU WASH MY BACK?

AS THEY ALWAYS SAY: YA SHOP TIL YA DROP!

HAVEN'T YOU EVER SEEN A FLAMINGO WITH FINS?

JULY

ALWAYS PROTECT YOUR BUNS IN THE RED HOT SUN!

SPIKE, IT'S TOO LATE. NOW YOU'RE SHARK BAIT!

JUST THINK, ONLY 300 DAYS TIL NEXT SUMMER!

BOO! BET YOU CAN'T GUESS WHO THIS IS?

LET'S TALK TURKEY!

WHO SAID SANTA ONLY LIKES MILK AND COOKIES?

GENERAL DIRECTIONS

1. Measure blocks and borders and add ¼" seam allowance to all. Cut fabric for blocks and borders. you may wish to add ½" all around and trim the blocks to fit after you finish the appliqués.

2. Tape pattern on a light box or window, center block fabric on pattern and trace with a mechanical pencil. Use a light touch and trace just outside pattern lines. This will make it easier to cover pencil lines when appliquéing. Remove fabric.

3. Place fabric for each appliqué piece on the light box or window. Trace just outside the pattern lines with a white chalk pencil. These lines should brush off after appliqué is finished. Cut out each piece adding ⅛" to ¼" seam allowance. "Crush" fabrics, textured hand-dyed fabrics, are suggested for some pieces.

4. Work the appliqués from the background to the foreground using your favorite appliqué technique. (Pieces which are under another piece should be appliquéd first.)

YARDAGE FOR FRONT OF QUILT

- 12 fat quarters in various colors for background of blocks
- 4 yds. white for 8" border and various blocks
- 4 yds. dark charcoal for border, silhouettes on large border, sashings and outer binding
- 1½ yds. light flamingo orange for sashing with hearts & mini flamingos
- 1 yd. teal for border
- 1 yd. red crush for outer border
- Approximately ½ yd. flamingo orange crush for flamingos
- ½ yd black crush for beaks, legs, etc.
- Mini rolls of following colors: pink, purple, blue, green, yellow, orange, brown and gray
- Scrap pieces of pieces above can be used for various items in blocks.

YARDAGE FOR BACK OF QUILT (WITH APPLIQUÉD DESIGN)

- 9 yds. muslin for background
- 2 yds. flamingo crush
- 1 yd. light flamingo crush
- 1 yd. pink crush
- ½ yd. black crush
- Various scraps from front may be used to make sneakers, shoes, and accessories on back.

Measurements given are finished size; add seam allowances when cutting. Full size block patterns are given on pages 24-71; just trace, putting the four quadrants together. Border patterns are given on page 23. The quilt back can be made plain, or can feature two large flamingos, as shown in the drawing on page 2. To make a back with this design, enlarge the border patterns on page 23 and add details of glasses, bows, sneakers, etc. Enjoy!

DIRECTIONS FOR SMALL QUILT

Blocks shown in small quilt are the actual size from the book (not enlarged to full size). The blocks were chosen from the pattern book so that one block represents one block from each season.

Flamingos on back of small quilt are the enlarged version of the silhouette border. Enlarge to 20" x 25".

Add ¼" seam allowance to all blocks and borders.

YARDAGE NEEDED:

- •1 fat quarter sky blue for February
- •1 fat quarter sky blue for April
- •1 fat quarter water blue for June
- •1 fat quarter purple for October
- •1 yd charcoal for sashing & binding
- •½ yd light flamingo crush for borders
- •1 fat quarter black crush
- •1 fat quarter flamingo crush
- •1 mini roll of green
- •1 mini roll of butterscotch
- •1 mini roll of purple
- •Scraps of yellow, pink, black and white
- •1 mini roll of red for flamingo and hearts around border.

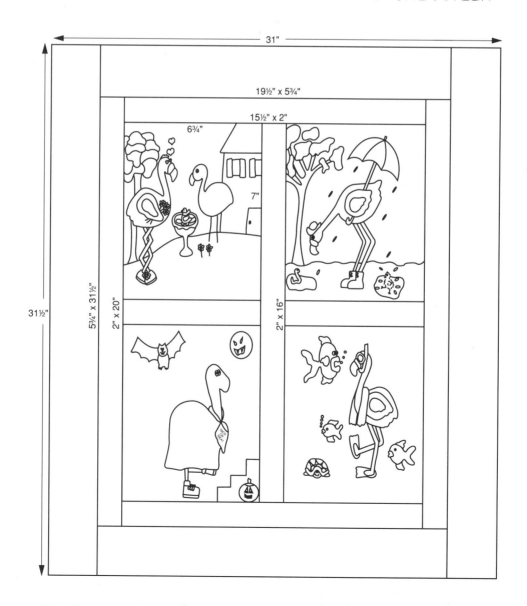

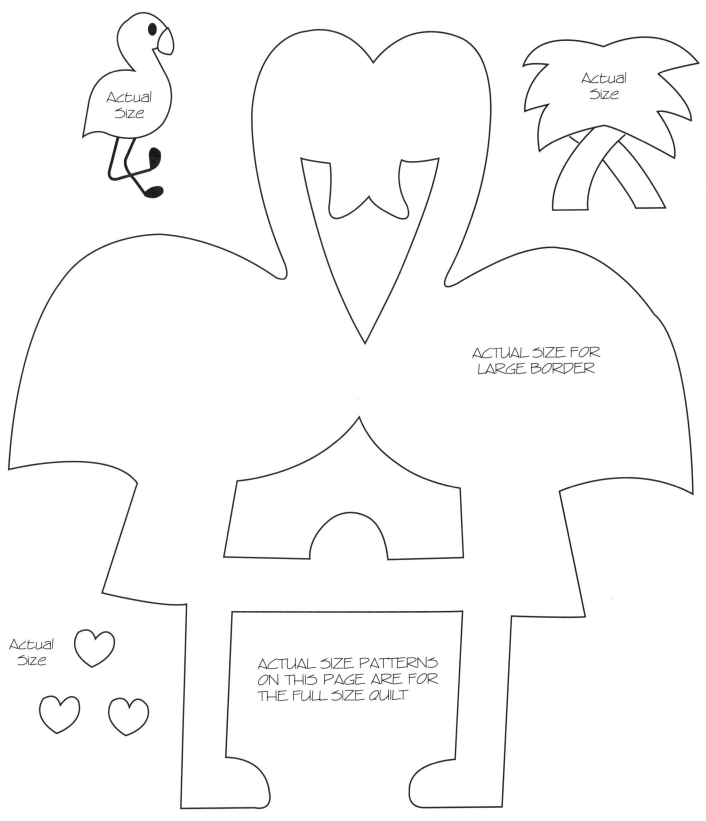

Actual Size

Actual Size

ACTUAL SIZE FOR
LARGE BORDER

Actual Size

ACTUAL SIZE PATTERNS
ON THIS PAGE ARE FOR
THE FULL SIZE QUILT

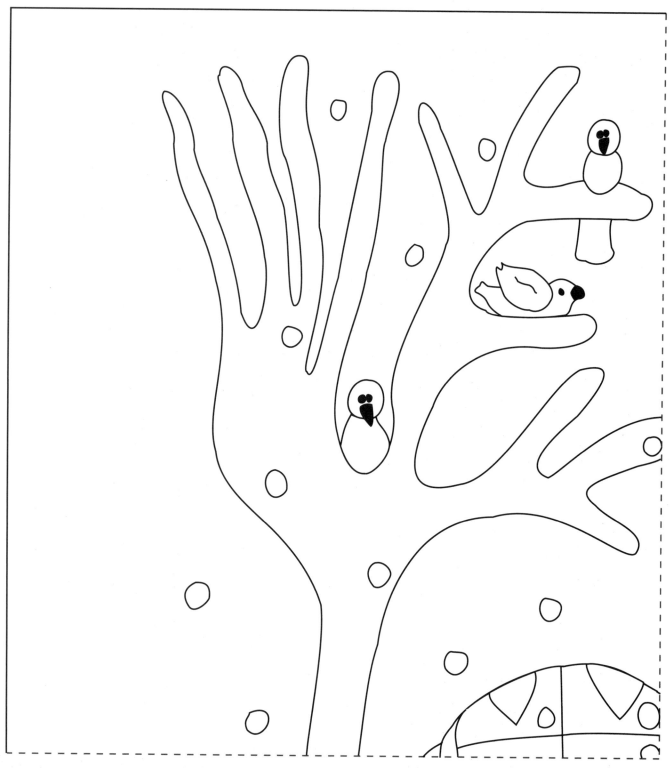

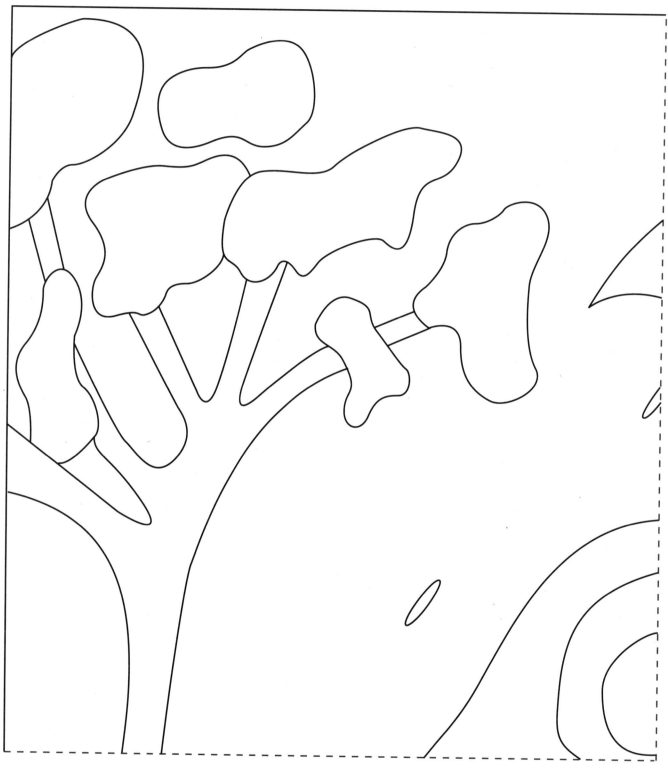

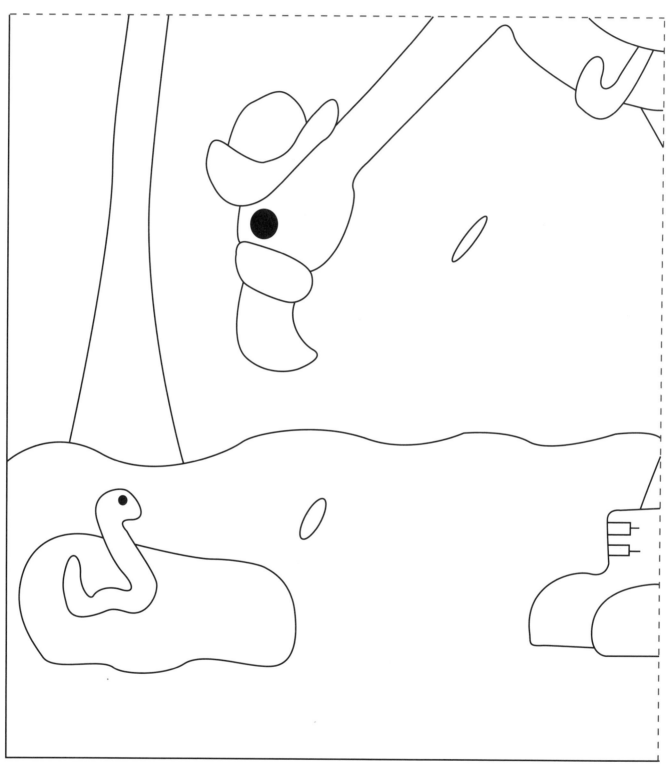

FLAMINGDALE

SALE

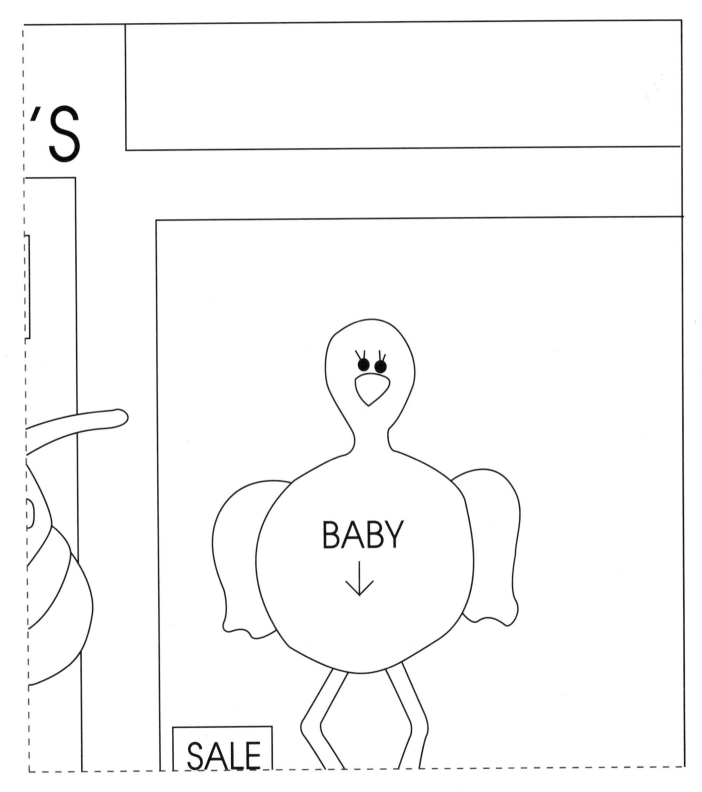

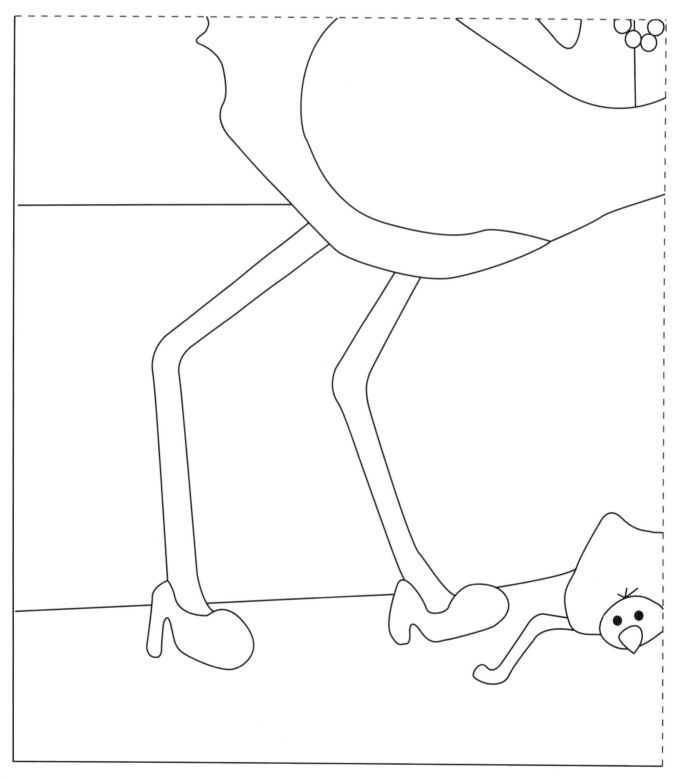

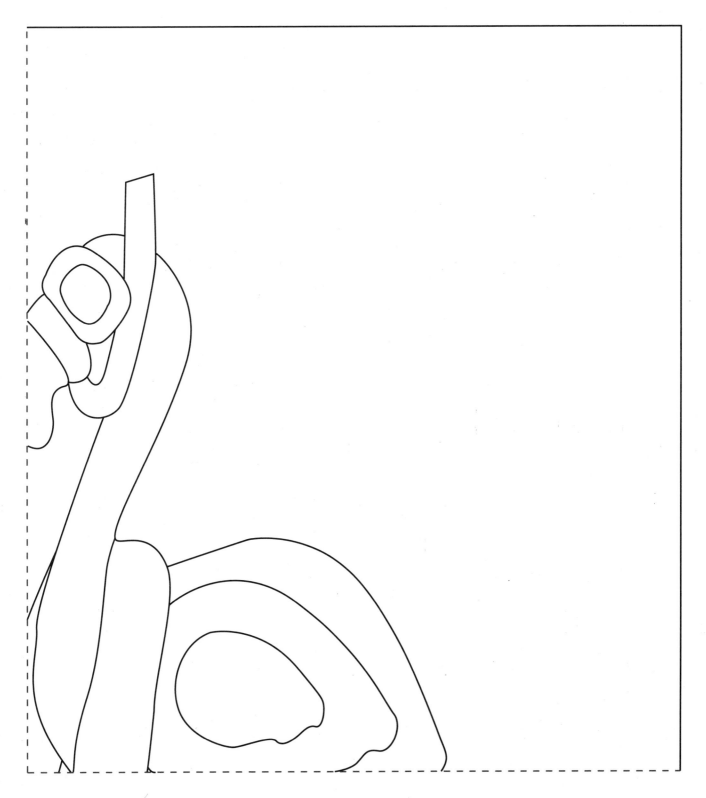

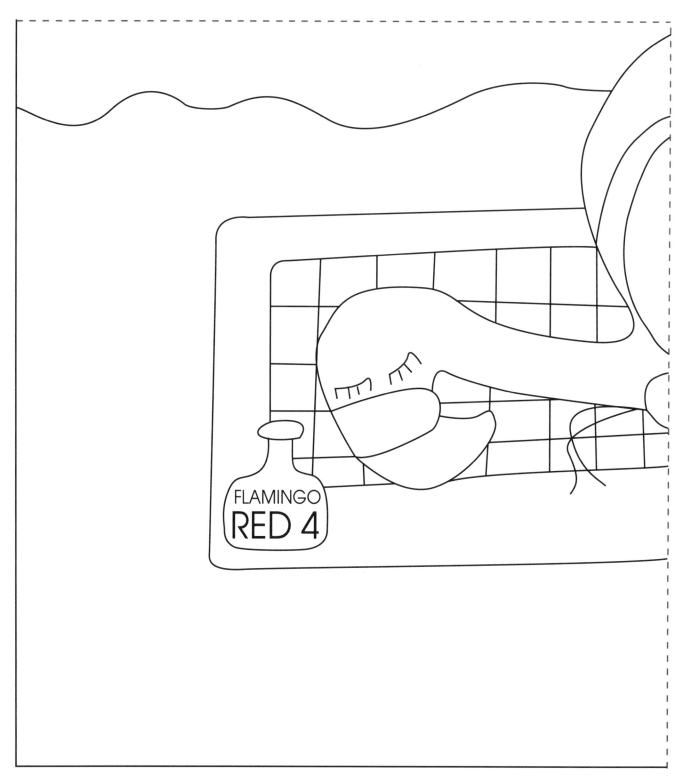

FLAMINGO
RED 4

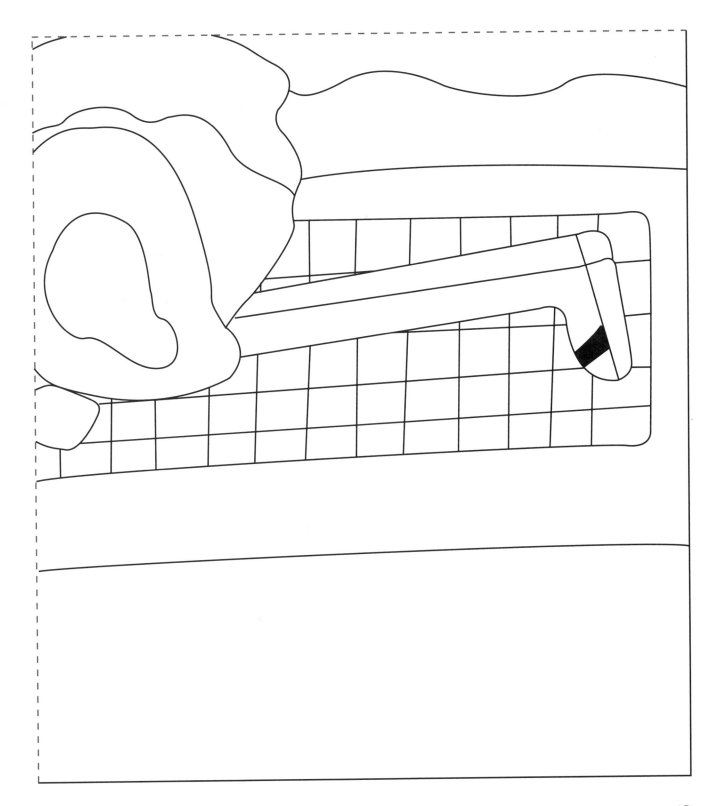

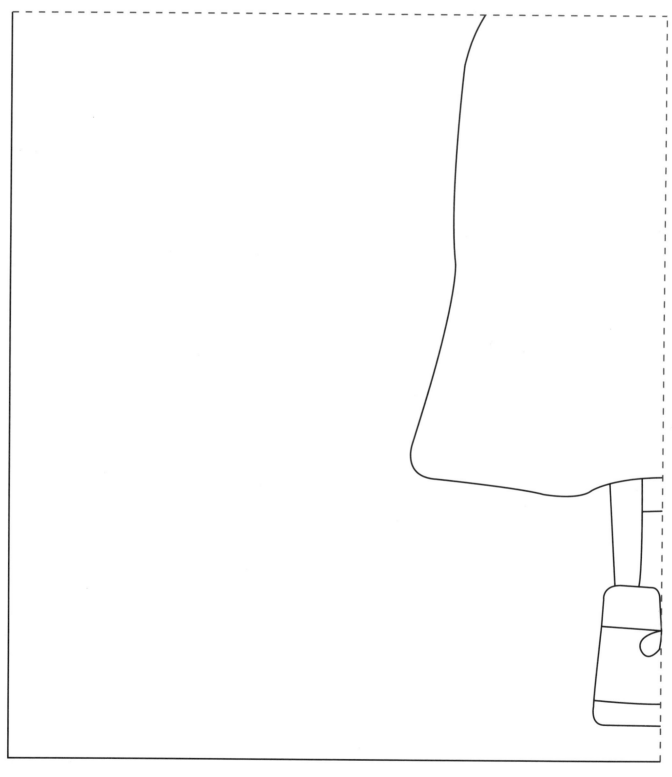

TRICK
OR
TREAT

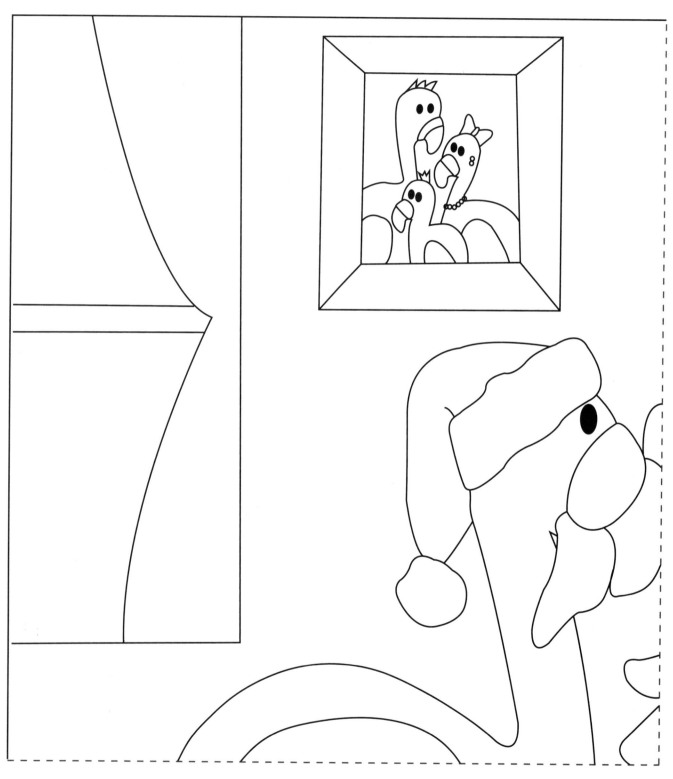

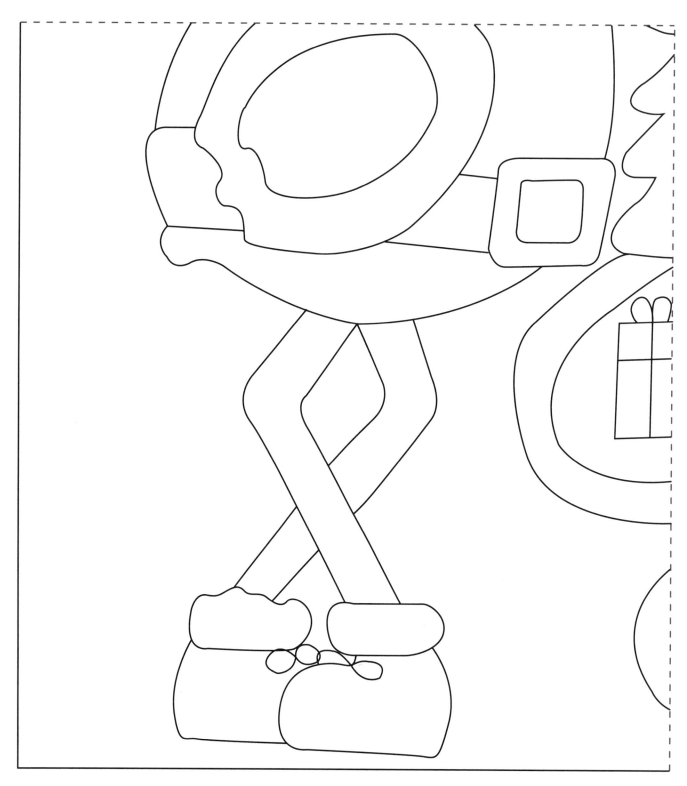

SANTA

∾ American Quilter's Society ∾
dedicated to publishing books for today's quilters

The following AQS publications are currently available:

- **Adapting Architectural Details for Quilts,** Carol Wagner, #2282: AQS, 1991, 88 pages, softbound, $12.95
- **American Beauties: Rose & Tulip Quilts,** Gwen Marston & Joe Cunningham, #1907: AQS, 1988, 96 pages, softbound, $14.95
- **America's Pictorial Quilts,** Caron L. Mosey, #1662: AQS, 1985, 112 pages, hardbound, $19.95
- **Applique Designs: My Mother Taught Me to Sew,** Faye Anderson, #2121: AQS, 1990, 80 pages, softbound, $12.95
- **Arkansas Quilts: Arkansas Warmth,** Arkansas Quilter's Guild, Inc., #1908: AQS, 1987, 144 pages, hardbound, $24.95
- **The Art of Hand Applique,** Laura Lee Fritz, #2122: AQS, 1990, 80 pages, softbound, $14.95
- **...Ask Helen More About Quilting Designs,** Helen Squire, #2099: AQS, 1990, 54 pages, 17 x 11, spiral-bound, $14.95
- **Award-Winning Quilts & Their Makers: Vol. I, The Best of AQS Shows – 1985-1987,** #2207: AQS, 1991, 232 pages, softbound, $24.95
- **Award-Winning Quilts & Their Makers: Vol. II, The Best of AQS Shows – 1988-1989,** #2354: AQS, 1992, 176 pages, softbound, $24.95
- **Award-Winning Quilts & Their Makers: Vol. III, The Best of AQS Shows – 1990-1991,** #3425: AQS, 1993, 180 pages, softbound, $24.95
- **Classic Basket Quilts,** Elizabeth Porter & Marianne Fons, #2208: AQS, 1991, 128 pages, softbound, $16.95
- **A Collection of Favorite Quilts,** Judy Florence, #2119: AQS, 1990, 136 pages, softbound, $18.95
- **Creative Machine Art,** Sharee Dawn Roberts, #2355: AQS, 1992, 142 pages, 9 x 9, softbound, $24.95
- **Dear Helen, Can You Tell Me?...all about quilting designs,** Helen Squire, #1820: AQS, 1987, 51 pages, 17 x 11, spiral-bound, $12.95
- **Dye Painting!,** Ann Johnston, #3399: AQS, 1992, 88 pages, softbound, $19.95
- **Dyeing & Overdyeing of Cotton Fabrics,** Judy Mercer Tescher, #2030: AQS, 1990, 54 pages, softbound, $9.95
- **Flavor Quilts for Kids to Make: Complete Instructions for Teaching Children to Dye, Decorate & Sew Quilts,** Jennifer Amor #2356: AQS, 1991, 120 pages, softbound, $12.95
- **From Basics to Binding: A Complete Guide to Making Quilts,** Karen Kay Buckley, #2381: AQS, 1992, 160 pages, softbound, $16.95
- **Fun & Fancy Machine Quiltmaking,** Lois Smith, #1982: AQS, 1989, 144 pages, softbound, $19.95
- **The Grand Finale: A Quilter's Guide to Finishing Projects,** Linda Denner, #1924: AQS, 1988, 96 pages, softbound, $14.95
- **Heirloom Miniatures,** Tina M. Gravatt, #2097: AQS, 1990, 64 pages, softbound, $9.95
- **Infinite Stars,** Gayle Bong, #2283: AQS, 1992, 72 pages, softbound, $12.95
- **The Ins and Outs: Perfecting the Quilting Stitch,** Patricia J. Morris, #2120: AQS, 1990, 96 pages, softbound, $9.95
- **Irish Chain Quilts: A Workbook of Irish Chains & Related Patterns,** Joyce B. Peaden, #1906: AQS, 1988, 96 pages, softbound, $14.95
- **The Log Cabin Returns to Kentucky: Quilts from the Pilgrim/Roy Collection,** Gerald Roy and Paul Pilgrim, #3329: AQS, 1992, 36 pages, 9 x 7, softbound, $12.95
- **Marbling Fabrics for Quilts** Kathy Fawcett & Carol Shoaf, #2206: AQS, 1991, 72 pages, softbound, $12.95
- **More Projects and Patterns: A Second Collection of Favorite Quilts,** Judy Florence, #3330: AQS, 1992, 152 pages, softbound, $18.95
- **Nancy Crow: Quilts and Influences,** Nancy Crow, #1981: AQS, 1990, 256 pages, 9 x 12, hardcover, $29.95
- **Nancy Crow: Work in Transition,** Nancy Crow, #3331: AQS, 1992, 32 pages, 9 x 10, softbound, $12.95
- **New Jersey Quilts – 1777 to 1950: Contributions to an American Tradition,** The Heritage Quilt Project of New Jersey; text by Rachel Cochran, Rita Erickson, Natalie Hart & Barbara Schaffer, #3332: AQS, 1992, 256 pages, softbound, $29.95
- **No Dragons on My Quilt,** Jean Ray Laury with Ritva Laury & Lizabeth Laury, #2153: AQS, 1990, 52 pages, hardcover, $12.95
- **Oklahoma Heritage Quilts,** Oklahoma Quilt Heritage Project #2032: AQS, 1990, 144 pages, softbound, $19.95
- **Old Favorites in Miniature,** Tina Gravatt, #3469: AQS, 1993, 104 pages, 8½ x 11, softbound, $15.95
- **Quilt Groups Today: Who They Are, Where They Meet, What They Do, and How to Contact Them; A Complete Guide for 1992-1993,** #3308: AQS, 1992, 336 pages, softbound, $14.95
- **Quilting Patterns from Native American Designs,** Dr. Joyce Mori, #3467: AQS, 1993, 80 pages, softbound, $12.95
- **Quilting with Style: Principles for Great Pattern Design,** Gwen Marston & Joe Cunningham, #3470: AQS, 1993, 192 pages, 9 x 12, hardbound, $19.95
- **Quiltmaker's Guide: Basics & Beyond,** Carol Doak, #2284: AQS, 1992, 208 pages, softbound, $19.95
- **Quilts: Old & New, A Similar View,** Paul D. Pilgrim and Gerald E. Roy, #3715: AQS, 1993, 40 pages, softbound, $12.95
- **Quilts: The Permanent Collection – MAQS,** #2257: AQS, 1991, 100 pages, 10 x 6½, softbound, $9.95
- **Seasons of the Heart & Home: Quilts for Summer Days,** Jan Patek, #3796: AQS, 1993, 160 pages, 8½ x 11, softbound, $18.95
- **Sensational Scrap Quilts,** Darra Duffy Williamson, #2357: AQS, 1992, 152 pages, softbound, $24.95
- **Show Me Helen...How to Use Quilting Designs,** Helen Squire, #3375: AQS, 1993, 155 pages, softbound, $15.95
- **Sets & Borders,** Gwen Marston & Joe Cunningham, #1821: AQS, 1987, 104 pages, softbound, $14.95
- **Somewhere in Between: Quilts and Quilters of Illinois,** Rita Barrow Barber, #1790: AQS, 1986, 78 pages, softbound, $14.95
- **Stenciled Quilts for Christmas,** Marie Monteith Sturmer, #2098: AQS, 1990, 104 pages, softbound, $14.95
- **A Treasury of Quilting Designs,** Linda Goodmon Emery, #2029: AQS, 1990, 80 pages, 14 x 11, spiral-bound, $14.95
- **Wonderful Wearables: A Celebration of Creative Clothing,** Virginia Avery, #2286: AQS, 1991, 184 pages, softbound, $24.95

These books can be found in local bookstores and quilt shops. If you are unable to locate a title in your area, you can order by mail from AQS, P.O. Box 3290, Paducah, KY 42002-3290. Please add $1 for the first book and 40¢ for each additional one to cover postage and handling. (International orders please add $1.50 for the first book and $1 for each additional one.)